THE
Little Book
— OF —
L O V E

D0914603

In the same series

THE
Little Book
— OF —
L O V E

E L E M E N T
Shaftesbury, Dorset ✦ Rockport, Massachusetts
Brisbane, Queensland

Compiled by John Baldock *with* Margaret Irvine

© ELEMENT BOOKS LIMITED 1994

Published in Great Britain in 1994 by
ELEMENT BOOKS LIMITED
Longmead, Shaftesbury, Dorset

Published in the USA in 1994 by
ELEMENT, INC
42 Broadway, Rockport, MA 01966

Published in Australia in 1994 by
ELEMENT BOOKS LIMITED
for JACARANDA WILEY LIMITED
33 Park Road, Milton, Brisbane, 4064
Reprinted 1996

Frontispiece: The Ardent Suitor by Hermann Vogler
Cover illustration: A Basket of Flowers by Jules Ferdinand Medard
Fine Art Picture Library

Designed by
BRIDGEWATER BOOKS
Typeset by VANESSA GOOD

Printed and bound in Italy by L.E.G.O.

British Library Cataloguing in Publication data available
Library of Congress Cataloging in Publication data available

ISBN 1-85230-471-5

Love is the most wonderful thing
in the world.

FRANÇOISE SAGAN

wonder, by my troth,
　　　what thou and I
Did till we loved?
　　　Were we not weaned till then?
But sucked on country pleasures childishly?
Or snorted we in the Seven Sleeper's den?
'Twas so; but this, all pleasures fancies be.
If ever any beauty I did see,
Which I desired, and got,
　　　'twas but a dream of thee.

JOHN DONNE, from *The Good-Morrow*

et us love one another: for love is of God; and every one that loveth is born of God, and knoweth God. He that loveth not knoweth not God; for God is love… and he that dwelleth in love dwelleth in God, and God in him.

1 JOHN 4:7-8, 16

I dare not ask a kiss;

   I dare not beg a smile;

Lest having that or this,

   I might grow proud the while.

*N*o, no, the utmost share

   Of my desire shall be

Only to kiss the air

   That lately kissèd thee.

ROBERT HERRICK, from *To Electra*

The madness of love
is the greatest of heaven's blessings.

PLATO, from *Phaedrus*

$\mathcal{G}$ive all to love;

     Obey thy heart.

RALPH WALDO EMERSON,

     from *Give All To Love*

She was sitting with her back to a window which was shaded by a white blind. A sunbeam filtering through the blind shed a gentle light on her soft golden hair, on her pure throat, on her tranquil breast... It seemed to me that I had known her for a long time, and that before her I had known nothing and had not lived... 'And here I am sitting opposite her,' I was thinking, 'I have met her; I know her. God, what happiness!' I almost leapt from my chair in ecstasy...

IVAN TURGENEV, from *First Love*

The countless generations
　　　　Like Autumn leaves go by:
Love only is eternal,
　　　　Love only does not die…

HARRY KEMP, from *The Passing Flower*

So well I love thee as without thee I
Love nothing; if I might choose,
I'd rather die
Than be one day debarred thy company.

MICHAEL DRAYTON

The great tragedy of life
is not that men perish, but that they
cease to love.

W. SOMERSET MAUGHAM

The attraction Madame de Clèves had for Monsieur de Nemours caused sensations over which she had no control. She realised that the most shaded remarks from a man of whom one is very fond can cause more agitation in one's heart than the most open declarations from a man for whom one feels no affection at all.

MADAME DE LAFAYETTE,

from *La Princesse de Clèves*

ow do I love thee?
       Let me count the ways.
I love thee to the depth and
       breadth and height
My soul can reach,
       when feeling out of sight
For the ends of Being and ideal Grace.
I love thee to the level of every day's
Most quiet need, by sun and candlelight.
I love thee freely,
       as men strive for Right;
I love thee purely,
       as they turn from Praise.

I love thee with the passion put to use
In my old griefs,
        and with my childhood's faith.
I love thee with a love I seemed to lose
With my lost saints -
        I love thee with the breath,
Smiles, tears, of all my life! -
        and, if God choose,
I shall but love thee better after death.

ELIZABETH BARRETT BROWNING,

from *Sonnets from the Portuguese*

Through love you can see God.

YOGASWAMI

$\mathcal{G}$od is love, and love is joy.
All the universe has come from love and
unto love all things return.

JUAN MASCARO

hatever you taste of love,

in whatever manner,

in whatever degree - it is a tiny part of

Divine Love.

SHEIKH MUZAFFER OZAK,

from *Love is the Wine*

Sally started coming up the stairs, and I started down to meet her. She looked terrific. She really did...
The funny part is, I felt like marrying her the minute I saw her. I'm crazy. I didn't even like her much, and yet all of a sudden I felt like I was in love with her and wanted to marry her.

J. D. SALINGER,

from *The Catcher in the Rye*

ove is, above all,

the gift of oneself.

JEAN ANOUILH

Our love looks boldly
    in the moon's bold eyes.
He has no thing to hide, no thing to fear.
And if the world stands far or hurtles near
He walks alway, serene, without disguise,
Naked and not ashamed beneath the skies.
He does not need dark backgrounds
        to appear
Radiant, for even through the broad
        day's clear
Effulgence his supernal beauties rise.
Oh, there be loves that hide
        till day is done:

Nocturnal loves, like silent birds of prey:
Secretive loves that do not dare rejoice.
Ours is an eagle that can face the sun.
A wholesome love that glories in the day,
And finds a rapture in its own glad voice.

ELLA WHEELER WILCOX, from *Threefold*

*O*h, life is a glorious cycle of song,

A medley of extemporanea;

And love is a thing

that can never go

wrong;

And I am Marie of

Roumania.

DOROTHY PARKER

A love song is just

a caress set to music.

SIGMUND ROMBERG

We are the dupes of myth
when we upbraid
Ourselves because we love;
for we are made
For loving: all the sweets of living are
For those that love. Be joyful, unafraid!

THE RUBAIYAT OF OMAR KHAYYAM

'Tis better to have loved and lost

Than never to have loved at all.

ALFRED, LORD TENNYSON

I love her with a love as still
    As a broad river's peaceful might,
Which, by high tower and lowly mill,
Seems following its own wayward will,
And yet doth ever flow aright.

JAMES RUSSELL LOWELL,

from *My Love*

All love at first, like generous wine,
Ferments and frets until 'tis fine;
But when 'tis settled on the lee,
And from th'impurer matter free,
Becomes the richer still the older,
And proves the pleasanter the colder.

SAMUEL BUTLER,

from *Miscellaneous Thoughts*

Stone walls do not a prison make,
    Nor iron bars a cage;
Minds innocent and quiet take
    That for an hermitage;
If I have freedom in my love,
    And in my soul am free;
Angels alone that soar above,
    Enjoy such liberty.

RICHARD LOVELACE,

from *To Althea, from Prison*

ove is my bait;
you must be caught by it;
it will put its hook into your heart and
force you to know that of all strong things
nothing is so strong, so irresistible,
        as divine love.
It brought forth all the creation;
it kindles all the life of Heaven;
it is the song of all the angels of God…
and from the beginning to the end of time
the one work of Providence is the one
work of love.

WILLIAM LAW

en always want to be a woman's first love; women have a more subtle instinct: what they like is to be a man's last romance.

OSCAR WILDE

ove one another, but make
not a bond of love:
Let it rather be a moving sea between the
        shores of your souls.
Fill each other's cup
        but drink not from one cup.
Give one another of your bread
        but eat not from the same loaf.
Sing and dance together and be joyous,
        but let each one of you be alone,
Even as the strings of a lute are alone
        though they quiver
with the same music.

KALIL GIBRAN, from *The Prophet*

Of all forms of caution,

caution in love

is perhaps the most fatal

to true happiness.

BERTRAND RUSSELL

or one human being to love another: that is perhaps the most difficult of all our tasks, the ultimate, the last test and proof, the work for which all other work is but preparation.

RAINER MARIA RILKE

earts and darts and maids and men,

   Vows and valentines are here;

Will you give yourself again,

   Love me for another year?

They who give themselves forever,

   All contingencies to cover,

Know but once the kind and clever

   Strategies of loved and lover.

Rather let the year renew

   Rituals of happiness;

When the season comes to woo,

   Let me ask, and you say yes.

JOHN ERSKINE,

Valentine To One's Wife

*W*hen you know you are loved
you have freedom.

RESHAD FEILD

My heart is like a singing bird
Whose nest is in a watered shoot;
My heart is like an apple-tree
Whose boughs are bent
with thick-set fruit;
My heart is like a rainbow shell
That paddles in a halcyon sea;
My heart is gladder than all these
Because my love is come to me.

CHRISTINA ROSSETTI,

from *A Birthday*

He who loves does not dispute:
He who disputes does not love.

LAO TZU

here is no fear in love;
but perfect love
casteth out fear.

1 JOHN 4:18

*U*nable are the Loved to die
For Love is Immortality,
Nay, it is Deity –

*U*nable they that love – to die
For Love reforms Vitality
Into Divinity

EMILY DICKINSON

et me not to the marriage of true minds
Admit impediments. Love is not love
Which alters when it alteration finds,
Or bends with the remover to remove.
O no, it is an ever fixèd mark
That looks on tempests
        and is never shaken;
It is the star of every wand'ring barque,
Whose worth's unknown although his
        height be taken.
Love's not Time's fool, though rosy lips
        and cheeks
Within his bending sickle's compass come;

Love alters not with his brief hours
          and weeks,
But bears it out even to the edge of doom.
If this be error and upon me proved,
I never writ, nor no man ever loved.

WILLIAM

SHAKESPEARE,

from

The Sonnets

$\mathcal{L}$ove alone is capable of
uniting human beings
in such a way
as to complete and fulfil them,
for it alone takes them and joins them by
what is deepest in themselves.

PIERRE TEILHARD DE CHARDIN

Lovers don't finally meet somewhere.
They're in each other
all along.

JALALU'DDIN RUMI,

from *Open Secret*

hen you are old and grey
    and full of sleep,
And nodding by the fire,
    take down this book,
And slowly read,
    and dream of the soft look
Your eyes had once,
    and of their shadows deep;

How many loved your moments
    of glad grace,
And loved your beauty
    with love false or true,

But one man loved the pilgrim soul in you,

And loved the sorrows

         of your changing face;

And bending down beside the glowing bars,

Murmur, a little sadly, how Love fled

And paced upon the mountains overhead

And hid his face amid a crowd of stars.

           W . B . Y E A T S , *When You Are Old*

ometimes with one I love
I fill myself with rage
for fear I effuse
unreturn'd love,
But now I think there is
no unreturn'd love, the pay is certain
one way or another,
(I loved a certain person ardently and my
love was not return'd,
Yet out of that I have written these songs.)

WALT WHITMAN,

Sometimes With One I Love

I love you, oh my darling,
        And what I can't make out
Is why since you have left me
        I'm somehow still about.

JOHN BETJEMAN,
from *The Cockney
Amorist*

he whole world
is a market-place for Love,
For naught that is,
      from Love remains remote.
The Eternal Wisdom made all things
      in Love:
On Love they all depend, to Love all turn.
The earth, the heavens, the sun,
      the moon, the stars
The centre of their orbit find in Love.
By Love are all bewildered, stupefied,
Intoxicated by the Wine of Love.

From each, a mystic silence Love demands,
What do all seek so earnestly? 'Tis Love.
Love is the subject of their inmost thoughts,
In Love no longer 'Thou' and 'I' exist,
For self has passed away in the Beloved.
Now will I draw aside the veil from Love,
And in the temple of mine inmost soul
Behold the Friend, Incomparable Love.
He who would know the secret
        of both worlds
Will find the secret of them both, is Love.

FARID AL-DIN ATTAR

$\mathcal{L}$ove is a conflict between

reflexes and reflections.

MAGNUS HIRSCHFELD

*L*ove is like the measles;

we all have to go through it.

JEROME K. JEROME,

from *Idle Thoughts of an Idle Fellow*

*L*ove is but the discovery of
ourselves in others,
and the delight in the recognition.

ALEXANDER SMITH

My love for Linton is like the foliage in the woods. Time will change it, I'm well aware, as winter changes the trees. My love for Heathcliff resembles the eternal rocks beneath – a source of little visible delight, but necessary. Nelly, I *am* Heathcliff – he's always, always in my mind – not as a pleasure, any more than I am always a pleasure to myself – but as my own being.

EMILY BRONTE, from *Wuthering Heights*

'Tis love, 'tis love,
that makes the world go round!

LEWIS CARROLL,

from *Alice's Adventures in Wonderland*

The fruit of the Spirit is love…

GALATIANS 5:22

ove is patient and kind; love is not jealous or boastful; it is not arrogant or rude. Love does not insist on its own way; it is not irritable or resentful; it does not rejoice at wrong, but rejoices in the right. Love bears all things, believes all things, hopes all things, endures all things. Love never ends...

1 CORINTHIANS 13:4-8

Acknowledgements

Permission to reproduce material protected by copyright has been sought in connection with the following quotations: extracts from the Authorized Version of the Bible (The King James Bible) the rights in which are vested in the Crown, from the Crown's Patentee, Cambridge University Press; Ivan Turgenev, *First Love*, translation © Isaiah Berlin 1950, published by Hamish Hamilton; Madame de Lafayette, *La Princesse de Clèves*, translation © J. Walter Cobb 1961, published by Signet Classics; Sheikh Muzaffer Ozak, *Love is the Wine*, © Robert Frager 1987, published by Threshold Books; J. D. Salinger, *The Catcher in the Rye*, © J. D. Salinger 1951, published by Penguin Books; Kalil Gibran, *The Prophet*, © Kalil Gibran 1923, © renewal 1951; Sir John Betjeman, *The Cockney Amorist*, © Estate of John Betjeman 1947, published by John Murray; Jalalu'ddin Rumi, *Open Secret*, © 1984 Threshold Books; W. B. Yeats, *When You Are Old*, published by MacMillan & Co; John Erskine, from *Sonata and Other Poems*, published by The Bobbs-Merrill Company; Harry Kemp, from *The Passing Flower*, published by Brentano's. Whilst every attempt has been made to obtain permission to reproduce material protected by copyright, where omissions may have occurred the compilers will be happy to acknowledge this in future printings of this book.

97!

I love you

Brenda

x